Verses n Sonnets

FRESHLY
Brewed

by Nupur

Quantity sales special discounts are available on quantity purchases by corporations, associations, and others. For details, contact the publisher at the address above.

Orders by U.S. trade bookstores and wholesalers. Email info@BeyondPublishing.net

The Beyond Publishing Speakers Bureau can bring authors to your live event. For more information or to book an event contact the Beyond Publishing Speakers Bureau speak@BeyondPublishing.net

The Author can be reached directly at BeyondPublishing.net

Manufactured and printed in the United States of America distributed globally by BeyondPublishing.net

BEYOND

New York | Los Angeles | London | Sydney

ISBN Hardcover: 978-1-637920-96-1

ISBN Softcover: 978-1-637920-97-8

Sit back and relax with your
favourite Cuppa..

Verses & Sonnets - A Journey

I started my writing journey 13 years ago and only started sharing my work on social media recently by launching the official handles of Verses & Sonnets. Back in the day, I would find myself writing as a way to channelize my feelings, emotions on any 'paper-like' thing I could find around me; be it the back of a restaurant feedback card, tissue paper, pages of an old notebook that had some empty space or even corners of visiting cards!

The reason? Because sometimes, when the words come to you - they just do and it's important to pen them down before they're forgotten. And so I did just that. I wrote and wrote and wrote some more.

The last few years have made me realise that words have become my 'go-to' person at most times in my life. The encouragement from readers who follow Verses & Sonnets on social media and have sent me overwhelming messages makes me smile.

I get teary when I read them as I am slowly
beginning to understand how the same words
are becoming a part of someone else's life too.

So here's celebrating all you amazing souls who
have always supported me and made Verses &
Sonnets what it is today. It's a milestone we all
celebrate together - to celebrate the power of words.

Verses & Sonnets - Freshly Brewed has been written
through countless experiences, observations and
finally finding a way of stringing words together to
bring out all those emotions and feelings.

A book that you can sit back, relax and read over
a nice cuppa! It should stir your emotions, make you
live the stories, live the moments through their highs
and lows.

I hope you enjoy reading this book as much as I
enjoyed putting it together!

Yours,
Nupur

To my amazing family..
Thank you for believing in me,
loving me unconditionally and always
encouraging me to be myself.

To the sunshine in my life..
That came out of nowhere..
Soaked me in it's warmth..
Patched me up bit by bit..
Made me love myself again..
To my stars and moon shining
brightly on me..
Thank you for lighting up my
darkest corners..
Thank you.. for everything..

MATTERS OF THE HEART

Love should be strong..
It should make you want to melt away
in its ecstatic feeling..
It should make you want to dance and
sway in it's madness...
Have that. That kind of love.
And when you find it, celebrate it
everyday because it's rarer than the
rarest diamond.

I'm yours. I love being yours.
I love saying that.
It's the most fulfilling feeling ever.
This sense of belonging.
That I can call someone in this
whole wide world mine
Just mine.

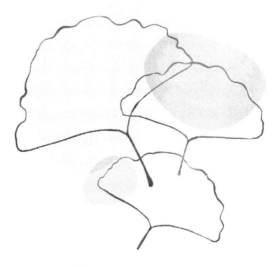

Sometimes I'm a total catastrophe
of emotions bursting from my very
core..
I don't know what gets over me..
but it does..
It's like an explosion.. of tears,
anger and betrayal..
But then I see you.. the calmness
on your face.. the warmth in your
eyes..
And with that loving look and that
gentle smile ..
When you invite me in your sweet
embrace..
All that pain just vanishes..
It's almost like the unsettling
outburst never existed..
And all I can see is you..
Just you..

Sometimes between what's said
and unsaid,
Between what's felt and what we
let go..
Between the turmoil that the heart
and mind create...
So much is left unfulfilled..
So much is simply left unfinished..

She ran to him with the burden of
emotions that filled up her chest..
Stopping in her tracks she looked
at him..
Hoping he'd say the right words..
the ones that heal her.. the ones
that make her whole again..
He looked at her, touching her soft
gentle cheeks and said "Come here
my love. Let me hold you. There's
so much to be grateful for. So
much to smile about. Just smile my
darling. It'll be okay"..
And so she melted into his arms...
As her cheeks let out that soft
smile he loved so much..

All she knew was how to love..
To give her all,
Give herself..
And then..
Give some more..

You'll always be the music
to my symphony..

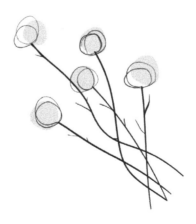

Let me drown in you until ..
All I can see is you..
All I can breathe is you..
Just you..

Whether or not you have someone
Whether or not, there ever will be
someone
Learn to love yourself first..
The rest can wait.

The yearning never really
stopped..
All she wanted was a little part of
him in her life..
In whatever form or way..
His presence made all the
difference ..
It's the only thing that kept
her sane ..
The only love that kept her going
That's all she truly desired..

He watched her run in the
sun-kissed field of corn..
But it was when she smiled and
laughed whole heartedly.. that he
knew..
How much he loved her, and..
What beauty really meant..

All she knows is that she's in love.
Love that can only be felt and be
written about..
A story that will make it to
chapters in history..
A love so pure that will inspire
others to believe in togetherness..
Yet a love, she knows can never
fully be hers..

Let me romance your craziness..
Drown in the depth of your eyes...
Melt away in your embrace..
Until we're both lost underneath..
While the stars gaze down
upon us..

She always found her voice and
was fierce about expressing her
feelings..
But when it came to him..no
matter what..
She was soft and gentle..
The rules always changed.. she
always bent them for him..
Always..

Say whatever you wish..
I'm in love..
I know what's coming..
And I know it'll hurt..
But I can't stop now..
That's just how I'm wired..

In her grim moments..love her..
When the skies are cloudy and
grey..
That's all that she really needs..

Love is a fragile word,
Often abused,
Taken for granted..
It's rarely truly and fully
understood..

Isn't it sad that most people don't really know the real meaning of true love?

She slept in peace only when she
wore his sweater to bed..
The softness of the fabric held her
close..
Almost like he was wrapping her
in his arms…
The smell of his cologne made the
closeness real..
She could almost feel his breath on
her skin ..

As I sat there alone.. trying to
keep it together..
A soft whisper beckoned saying,
"I'm holding you tight my darling,
it's going to be okay"

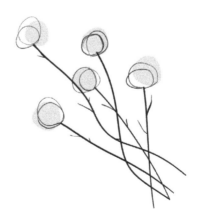

And sometimes, lost in the thought
of being in your arms..
My lips curve just a little and I
find myself smiling..

There is magic in every first..
The first time you touch..
The first time you kiss..
The first time you hug..
The first time.. will always be
special..

I'm so crazy in love..
It's like a spell,
I live him..
I breathe him..
I am one with him..

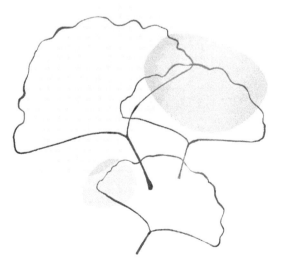

Is it crazy to want him every
second?
Is it crazy to think about him at
every waking hour?
Is it crazy to want to feel his touch
even if we're just next to each
other?
Is it crazy to drown in his eyes?
Do they call it crazy to fall in love
all over again..everytime he
smiles?
How crazy can crazy really be?
And if this is crazy.. then yes,
I am proudly crazy..

In the darkest room..
Or even in the dimness of the
night..
He had eyes only for her..

You are my breath of fresh air..
How can I ever live without you..
I'm so addicted to this love.. to
you.. to this feeling of being
yours.. to the idea of calling you
mine..
A love that drives me crazy..
A love that keeps me warm..
A love that's hard to find..
I'm so scared of losing it all..
losing you..
And being lost all over again.

I was drowning already,
But you came along and helped me
breathe underwater..

I'll always remember the day,
when he walked in.. and all the
darkness slowly began to fade
away..
There was music in the breeze
again.. there was a scent of
freshness around me..
And I suddenly remembered what
it felt like to smile again.. because
all my answers were there.. right
in front of me.. staring at me as he
stretched out his hand..
Waiting to introduce himself.
And I slowly obliged.. meeting his
palm with mine.

Some love stories are written in the stars.
The ones we can see every night.
And some are written in the stars that lie beyond.
The ones that do exist but can't be seen.
And perhaps never will.

When we saw each other for the
first time, let's go back there..
start again and do it right this
time..

It's easy to love her..
She doesn't need much..
Just companionship, sensitivity and
a cup of coffee..

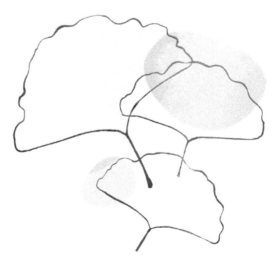

My heart said "Listen".. and so I
did..
It said, "Follow me".. and so I
did..
So here I am now, because it led
me to you..

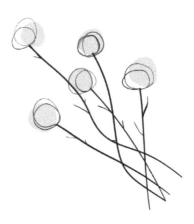

You'll always be the music
to my symphony..

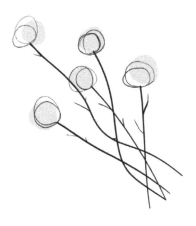

I love you.
A little more everyday.
Always and forever...

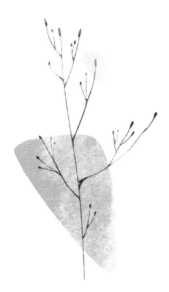

You've found real love when
someone decides to help split the
weight of the baggage you carry..

He was her Lion..
And she was his roar..

When you lock your eyes with
someone.. and your heart races
just that little bit..
Your lips curve into a smile just
that little bit..
The one that makes your breath
pace up just that little bit..
The one where you look away, all
shy..
That. Hold on to that

Call me crazy,
But this is the only way I know to
love..

The safest place in this universe is right here.. in your arms..

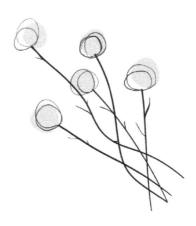

That moment was perfectly
divine.. When our eyes were
locked and fingers entwined..

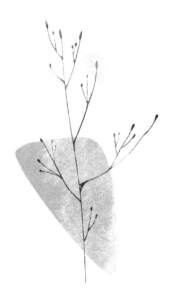

I will always give you my all..
Perhaps much more than I ever
give myself..
And it's because I love you
unconditionally..

The soft curly tresses falling down
her cheek,
The delicate curves around her
neck,
Her shoulders standing tall and
wide,
The smile that she wears that
brightens up her face,
The warmth in her deep eyes
shining through,
Is just the way he'd always
imagined her..

I don't know who you are..
All I know is I'm waiting for you,
My heart is gentle and my love is
pure..
When you come, I'll give myself to
you..
Be careful, I bruise easily
But I love unconditionally..

She's the fire that burns within my
soul,
Her laughter makes me complete
and whole..
Her eyes speak a thousand words,
For her smile, I'd lash countless
swords,
When she walks, time stands still
How I pray my wish is her will
If only she knew; our journey
would unfold,
Ours is a story of love untold..

Calculated love has no value,
Love should be passionate, crazy,
insanely irresistible,
Your soul should burst with thirst.
When you love so much, that you
feel it in every cell of your body..
That's when you've truly loved..

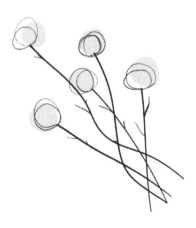

What we have,
No poem can capture..
No melody can describe..
It's a feeling inside you and I,
A feeling of unbelievable rapture..

It's really simple,
For me, you're my epitome of
love..

I'm a dreamer,
Be it day or night,
My visions, I hold with pride,
That's why I know what my heart
truly desires..

All we really need in this whole
wide world..
Are a pure pair of eyes..
One's that see through all the
masks..
The fake smiles...
And see us, for who we really are..

One's gentle heart..
Can heal another's broken soul..

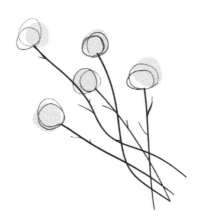

You and I will always have our
forever love..

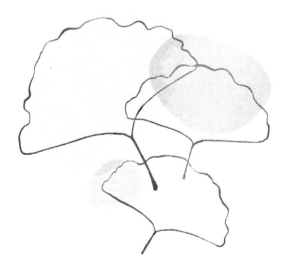

THE HURT AND THE PAIN

It's happening.. again..
I'm losing myself.. again..
And I don't know how to stop it..
Just this time .. don't let me
break..
For there will be nothing left of
me..
Nothing left to collect of myself
and put together again..

"What is it that you'd want me to grant you?.." asked that divine voice
"Just one thing" she said, unable to meet his gaze..
"Tell me.." He replied calmly..
"I'm hurting. My heart's aching. Please just make it stop."

I don't like this feeling..
It eats me from within..
It consumes me..
It becomes me..
This is not me..
Who am I?

The pain.. it comes and goes..
Some days are dark and gloomy..
Others bask in the rays of the sun..
Through it all.. tell yourself that
it's going to get better..
Nothing lasts forever..

Set me free..
Let me run..
Till I'm tired and out of breath..
And then..
I'll run some more...
Until I'm convinced I'm far far
away..

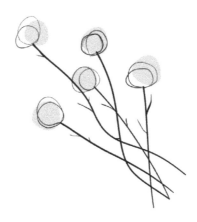

With the rain today..
Let me melt in its downpour..
Let me be washed away..
Let me become one with Mother
Earth again..
Let me be the dust..
Let me disappear.. just disappear..

Her eyes welled up with that one song.. again..
She knew the words .. but she couldn't get herself to sing them..
All she could see.. was that dark long road which lit up with fireflies..again..
All she could hear were the cries of two innocent souls.. scared and panicked..again..
All she knew, was the one person she loved the most.. was broken and shattered..again

I know you're broken too..
Pieces of you cut through my skin
as I walk towards you..
But I love you so much..
I am yours as you are mine..
At the cost of being slashed by
their sharpness, I'll walk towards
you anyway..

I just need some quiet..
A place where my mind finds
nothing to think about..
Like a box that's empty.. a
moment where I'm blank..
These thoughts are overbearing..
they weigh me down..
I just need some peace.. just a little
bit ..

It feels like there are ants crawling
on you.. all over you..
It feels like someone ripped your
heart out..
Like someone made a joke of your
very existence..
Like someone just took away every
inch of happiness you spent years
collecting, bit by bit..
Like nothing matters anymore..
Your pulse races.. everything is
moving so fast yet so slow..
Everything that made sense
doesn't anymore.
You can't hear your own voice..
You can't hear anyone else..
It's like a deep dark black hole and
you're sinking in.. just sinking in..
These demons feed on us every
now and then..
And I know them all too well..
Their names?
Anxiety and Depression..

It's funny how sometimes we feel like strangers even in the most familiar of surroundings.

Somehow..
We became two people who no
longer recognised each other..
Somehow..
The reasons seemed lost..
Somehow..
We grew apart..
Somehow..
It's all really over..

I feel you all the time..
Your breath, your lips, your
fingers..
Your memories are my thoughts..
Your voice still stops me in my
tracks..
Like an endless chant in my head..
Please release me.. free my soul..
Let me go..

Who are you?
And why don't I recognise you?
Where did the person I fell in love
with go?
What did you do to him?

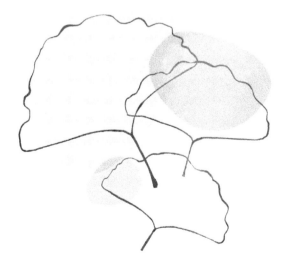

What's wrong? Asked a friendly
voice..
"I just wanted it to workout" she
said..

In the dark..
It's quiet..
The wind blows ever so slightly..
As she sits on the porch in her
rocking chair.. and a faint piano
sound.. somewhere afar..
Brings it all back.. the moments..
the memories..
That's when it happens..
A little twinge inside her chest..
Her cheek feels cold as a tear rolls
down..
And then it hits..
That soft pain..

I've felt it..
When someone's sucked out all the
good from around you and inside
you..
When you hear the waves of
sadness hitting the shores of your
heart..
And you want to run but there's
no where to go..
And you want to scream but
there's no one to listen..
Believe me, it's real and that shit is
hard

For every dream we dreamed
together and you broke..
For every promise we made and
you didn't keep..
For every moment you swore we'd
live..
For all the priceless blessings we
had and you never valued..
For all this.. I just have one
question..
Why? Why did you do it?

I know how much you love him. I know. I feel it. I can tell how your voice picks up pace and your face wears a subtle smile when you talk about him. And then again how it slowly fades away because I'm the only one you can share all this with. I know you've loved before. But this is different. This is magical. This feels complete. This is what it always should've been.

And now when you look back, it seems like what you thought was love was just infatuation that needed definition. A sense of comfort you felt you had when really, it was toxic and nothing else. But this. This is the real deal. I know. Your heart feels like it's in the right place, in the right hands. Where it belongs. A familiar feeling engulfs it, while it's still all so new. I know.

But I also know those sleepless nights, where you pray that now that you have this, it isn't snatched away. That it doesn't disappear like most things have in your life. Like making yourself immune again to the feeling of loss. I know.

I feel your shivers. I feel your cold hands. I see the worry in those eyes. I do. I know you never want to tell yourself again to move on because you know you've reached your destination. The last stop. It's here. I know. I feel how tightly you hug your pillow pretending to protect this love. I feel you darling. Just know that your love is pure and it really is what it is. There's nothing more you can do or pray for. Your heart doesn't allow you to feel freely. Your innocent mind doesn't let you run in liberation. I know. I get it. I really do. You're scared it'll all go away in a snap. And that empty feeling will creep in again. I hear your heart thumping hard against your chest even now just with the thought of that. No, this doesn't make you weak. It makes you a warrior who was brave enough to love again. I'm here with you. We are one. I don't know the future but I'm here with you. Always.

Love, Your Subconscious

It's just those few times, when the heart whispers, "yes I'm strong, but it'd be nice to belong to someone, for the world to see, wouldn't it?"..
And that's perhaps the only time when.. in this classic debate of love, the mind has nothing to say..

I don't want to live in the fear of
losing you someday.
But apparently of late that's all I do,
forgetting that I'm in the present, too
worried about what the future holds.
How do I stop this?
The thoughts are overbearing. They
eat me up from within..
Like I've no soul to feel..
No heart left to love..
I go cold and numb..
When did it get like this?

Let it happen. Do it once and for all. Don't say you're moving on if you're not ready to. Don't say you're okay if you're not. So allow it to happen. Just this one time. Let bit by bit of you break. Let all of your pieces fall. Set yourself free just this once from the expectation of being a Hero. Let those memories, those dreams, those hopes shatter once and for all. Once they have; give them a long stare. A long one. Of all the things that you expected. Of the failures. Of lost love. Of promises. Of hopes pinned to the stars. Take it all in. Because it's gone, and bid goodbye to the part of you that went with it. And then, when you're finally one with yourself, in the soundless night...

When you can finally hear your breath. And shut out the screams. When the tears have all dried up. Stand up, and walk away from all of this. Don't turn. Don't stop. Don't you dare look back again. Just walk and keep walking. And then, for the first time in your life, let the healing finally begin - once and for all. The true healing in every sense because you've really let it 'all' go.
To bring out the best version of you. Scarred, tired yet more determined than ever. It's you all the same. Yes. That one.
Be proud. Stand tall.

You finally did it.

Not all wars are in your face.
Some are being fought in the silence of
the night.
Others in the chaos of the day.
And most are the ones that go
unspoken of, because no one will ever
know they existed..
The ones in our head..

There it was. From a distance she could tell. One glimpse at it and she knew it was the shell. Her shell. Which kept her warm. Kept her quiet. Kept all those demons inside. Kept her sane. It's calling out to her. She knows this calling. She knows it so well. She's been here before. Hearing it call her name. Time and again. Sooner or later it's going to happen. Her world, her whole universe is going to come crashing down. She knows it. She can feel it. It's so close. It happens all the time. She knows once she goes back in there, it's going to take a long time before she can be herself again. People call her names. Drama Queen. Too sensitive. Too dreamy. The labels don't end. Her head is heavy with thoughts.

Make it stop. Make it go away.

Nowadays, it almost seems like the
smallest of things make the biggest
difference to my life. The most
inconsequential of things hurt.
Perhaps they shouldn't affect me as
much. Is it happening on its own or
am I allowing it to leave a footprint? I
really don't know.
Perhaps I need to build that wall
again. Because I know it kept me safe.
A fortress filled with a million rooms,
of which I could choose the farthest
one, to keep myself sane and
unscathed..
Maybe that's the only way..

In my book, please be the name that appears in every chapter and every page..

I try, I really do..
I try everyday..
But it's not working..
Something's just not right..
Every attempt falls short.. every try
falls flat..
I'm stuck.. What do I do?

Maybe all we need is the comfort of a
love that we can give freely ..
and receive without asking..

More often than not, for the constant turmoil in our heart and mind.. all we really seek are some answers for a concept we know as 'closure' ..

People take away things from you..
Only because somewhere, at some
point
You allowed them to..

It takes a second to break someone's heart, but a lifetime to put it back together again..

Her eyes speak to me..
Their depth proves her struggle..
The tears prove her might..
But above all is that fierce glare..
Portraying the conviction she has
and that she will never give up
without a fight..

Allow your pain to surface, don't
curb it
Allow for it's validation, don't shy
away
Allow for time to run it's course,
don't hurry
There is no winning formula to heal
It's only you, who can figure this
out..

The screams inside her get louder..
The voices inside her head grow
stronger..
Fighting her will. Fighting herself.
Taming her darkness.
She knows that to fight this, that
sword must come out again..

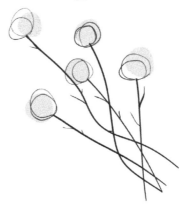

If you observe closely you'll realise
that time doesn't heal..
Time only helps you cope better..

The warrior that she was,
Whenever she looked in the mirror..
She was proud to see the face that
defeated all the demons inside her..

With each deep cut..
You learn to feel,
You learn to heal..
And then something changes..
Sometimes, forever..

Some of us are permanently
damaged,
And temporarily sane..
For only we can see and understand
our sea of pain..

Maybe I'm old and weak,
Maybe too much time has gone by,
But all I want, are her gentle fingers
on my cheek, and her soft voice
saying, "You did well. It's going to
be fine"

If you're lost,
let the stars be your saviour..

Don't blame the rain…
Because there are times..
Just those few..
When even the Gods need to cry..

Every tear stained pillow has a story
to tell..

Please be the air in my lungs,
everytime I choke up?

We put up a brave front..
Deal with everyday as if, a war..
Take the bullets head on, as life unfolds..
Swear to never give up..
But when the night comes and we are all alone with our vulnerability..
All we hear is the sound of our own breath..
Conscious of our being, we break..
We succumb to our wounds..
And then in a small corner of our heart..
It hurts..
And then it hurts some more..

I will fight,
I will conquer..
I will exult.
I will fall..
I will rebuild..
For these scars won't last..
They won't pull me down..
I won't let them..

You know me, yet you don't know
me
I have a dark side, a beast kept in
isolation..
A monster who cannot surface
among living beings..
A venom that's waiting to be
expelled..
No. It wasn't born with me. It was
born with situations. It fed on hurt,
tears and injustice..
I just need to find a way to contain
it, while it continues to feed itself
inside me..

She knows she's a force of nature..
A fighter..
Yet, why is it that when she needs it
the most..
She can't find her voice

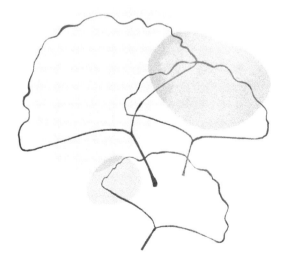

We see so much..
We know so much..
Yet..
We falter so much..

Better together
Disaster apart..

Disaster together
Better apart..

Which one are you?

I know it hurts..
I also know it will stop..

THE UPS
AND
DOWNS

He came like the freshness of the breeze..
Bringing with him all the positivity..
Sweeping me away from my emotional misery..

The only comfort she sought was
to hear his voice say..
"Smile. It's all about the sunshine
in your mind"

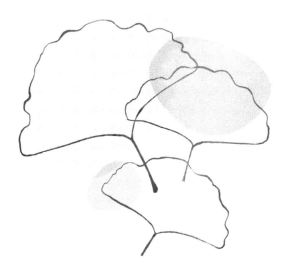

Like the clouds that cover the
softness of the moonlight..
Like the leaves that hold their little
fruit from the harsh wind..
Like the oyster that protects the
Pearl within..
That's how I imagine it..
Your warm embrace..

I can see it coming..
I can smell it..
The air is moist...
The sky is getting darker..
Clouds closing in..
And there it comes..
A drop at a time.. weighing down
on flowers..
Making their nectar sweeter..
As we dance away in this rain..

Feed your soul the warmth of the
sun..
The freshness of the wind..
The hope of the stars..
And the soft touch of a dream
called love..

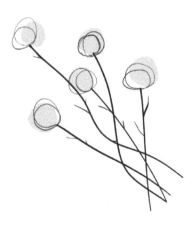

Time means nothing when I'm
with you.
It's like everything is exactly
where and how it's supposed to
be..
Like everything in the world is
okay and nothing can ever go
wrong..

Smile.
The stars are smiling down at you.
Something good is about to
happen.
Soak the sparkle in.

She smiles through her eyes..
With the sound of happiness in her
voice..
And the sense of contentment in
her breath..

I had a dream..
The world was exactly how it
should be..
There was peace..
The sun was shining brightly...
And finally in my subconscious,
deep within my core..
I felt what it really meant to be
happy..

They say it's hard to see the Silver
lining,
They say that people fail and in
their misery don't stop whining,
It's difficult to be positive always,
it is true..
And so it's possible that one's
always feeling Blue..
It's the moment when you decide
to wriggle out of your sadness..
The reminder of your will power to
drive you out of your own
madness..
For the Grey clouds do pass, and
church bells do ring..
There's a reason why even caged
birds sing..

The closer we see the world,
The more we realise that
'Happiness' isn't free,
It comes at a cost..
That's a fact..

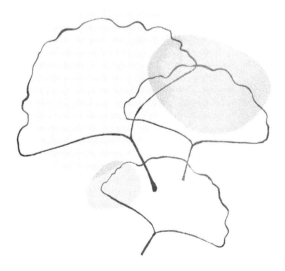

"When will I be happy", I asked,
"You will be and soon," said Life..
"You always say that," I
shrugged..
"Know your true worth first, then
you will know the meaning of
happiness," said Life..

Cheer up little angel,
It's finally happening..
Your life is about to change..
This time for the good..

It's wonderful to keep everyone
happy..
But sometimes, just for your sake..
Remember to keep yourself happy
first..

Just be...
Don't let them take away what's
yours..
This is you..
Celebrate yourself..

Stop feeding your demons
Let life take over..
It doesn't always have to be bad..

Haven't you noticed already?
All we're chasing, every single
day..is some peace, love and a little
magic called 'Happiness'..

Take a moment, breathe..
Look up and say 'Thank You'..
Because at the end of the day..
There's a magic in being
Grateful..

'You' are your own
Silver lining..

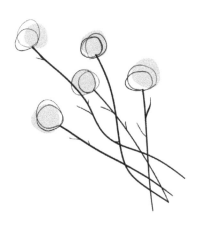

Solitude is the best teacher to help you understand the value of what you've been blessed with..

Don't shed any tears on things that
don't give you peace of mind..
Do you know how precious those
pearl drops are?
Instead, save them for a
heartwarming moment,
And let them roll down your
cheeks with nothing less than
pride..

Live, as if you'll die tomorrow..
Love, as it truly evades your
sorrows..
Cry, you'll feel lighter..
Express, your day will seem
brighter..
Forgive, for there's no bigger
bliss..
Feel, for there's always someone
you miss..
Breathe, it's the fuel to your life..
Live..
Just live..

There will come a time,
When the only things that will
matter are..
How much you've loved..
How deep your relationships run..
And how many blessings you've
collected along the way..
Despite the scars you bear, how
forgiving you've been..
And above all, the peace of mind
you have..

We fall only to rise again..
So everytime those hands are ready
to wave the 'White flag'..
Tell yourself to hang in there, one
more time..
You owe it to yourself..
You've come this far..

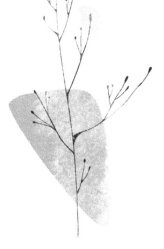

When the journey seems long..
Sit back and enjoy the scenery..
Watch those trees, the dark
tunnels, enjoy the breeze..
Sometimes, life has a way of
surprising you..
You just might catch a glimpse of
that magical rainbow..

I'd rather you hold me tight..
Than gift me rings..
I'd rather you let me be..
So I spread my wings..

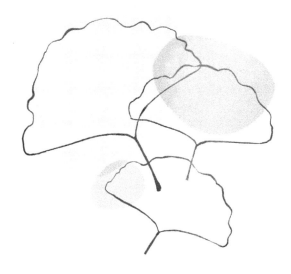

Sometimes,
All we really need..
Is some hope, or a short prayer..
Or perhaps a sonnet an angel sings
somewhere…

When everything around seemed hazy, and the grime settled around me..
When I walked through the corridors of a house unvoiced,
You found me..

When uncertainty clouded my thoughts,
And the rainbow of my dreams faded slowly, when I could hear a cry from a street called 'Solitude'..
You found me..

When my strength decided to vacate..
And all I could do is close my eyes and pray..when my dreams seemed like a distant memory..
You found me..

What if, in a parallel world..
Chaos meant peace..
Crazy meant genius..
Home was in the open and under
the stars..
Hugs were currency..
And the only punishable sin was to
be deprived of love?
What a wonderful world that
would be..

Smile, as it doesn't cost a penny,
Smile, so you can be a ray of hope
to someone dear,
Smile when your mind wanders
down memory lane..
Smile, because this very minute
someone is thinking of you..
Smile, because you're alive..
Just smile..

Be the unstoppable fire,
Be the unquenchable desire..
Be your own force..
Don't ever have remorse..
For someday they will read your
tale..
In a book so fancy that it goes up
for sale..

When things go wrong,
Don't get disheartened,
It's much easier to set them right..
When your soul is filled with
sunshine..
So just be glad..
It's the best way out..

When we say, living in the 'now'
It means 'now', this very moment
So take it in, soak it up,
Breathe and release..

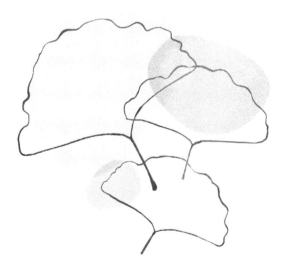

At first it hurts,
Then it hurts less..
Then along the way, the tears
don't sting..
The muffled cry softens..
And somewhere in the quiet..
You feel nothing, zilch..
That's when you know you're
immune..

Because in the end..
No matter what we say..
No matter what we do..
Kay Sera Sera..

You know you felt it..
And yet you ignore it..
You know you want it..
And yet you deny it..
Someday, you'll be sure you need
it..
But, it maybe too late to wish it..

The number of people who come to
pay their respects at your funeral
define the kind of life you've
lived..
Every blessing from them is a
brick laid in your stairway to
heaven..

We will probably take more than a
lifetime to figure out, how to
collect the pieces of ourselves.. lost
in our life, lost to things most
important to us.. and to the people
we once loved..

The only sword you should wear is
the one called 'Intelligence'..
The sharpest and the one that
slashes like no other..

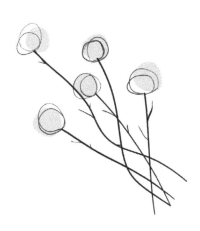

Signs, they come and go..
More often than not, they're
around us..
It's all about when you decide to
stop and look,
to understand, and take your next
step..

It only takes a few seconds to
destroy what took years to build..
Value what you have..

Be patient.. because..
What's meant for you,
Will come to you..

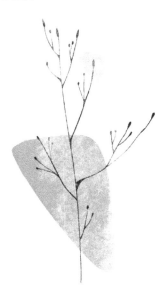

If all the answers you're looking for get answered, have you wondered what you'll do next?

Remember, what you say or speak
is yours,
How deep and where it manifests
isn't..

Emotional dependency comes from trust,
Just because someone was incapable of keeping that trust intact doesn't make you an emotional fool..

Unfinished stories in this life are a
page in your book, marked with a
bookmark that reminds you to
re-open it in another lifetime..

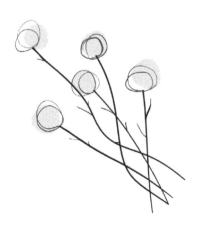

The day you make them realise
that they don't affect you
anymore..
You'll know strength in a way
you've never known before..
Let today be that day..

Going home to something or someone should always be worth it..

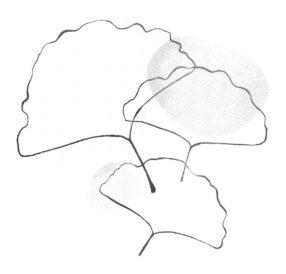

Because it still matters, it hurts
Because you still care, it stings
Because you still feel, your eyes
moisten..
You are human and empathetic..
A quality slowly diminishing in
our world..
So be proud of being you..

You are brave
You are driven
You have purpose
You're a masterpiece
Know that everyday

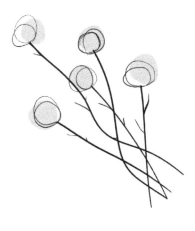

KEEPING IT REAL

I know I'm strong.
I also know I bruise easily.
I know I can overcome.
I also know that the process may
hurt.
I know I'm a force of nature.
It may take sometime to accept
things, and that can come with it's
own bag of emotions.
And so for all of the above, I have
no regrets.
For all of the above, I'm grateful.

"Don't do it".. said the mind..
"It's worth a try".. nudged the
heart

She was fierce.. with an exquisite
power..
The hardest shell on the outside..
The softest heart on the inside..
I know why I lost her..
But I don't know how I let it
happen..

I wish I could make a rhythm for
my life..
With each good moment as a high
note..
And each difficult moment as a
low note..
Wonder what that tune would
sound like?

We are all lost in the whirlwind of
life..
No real direction, but trying to
make each day count..
No real reason, but trying to give
each moment meaning..
No real hope, but holding it
together with the eagerness of a
better sunrise..

Admit it.
You're lost.
There's no shame in accepting
that.
You can't comprehend everything.
You've forgotten your self.
But soon enough you'll know, that
you are simply under a big cloud..
And once it passes it will all be
clear again..

Sometimes, it's important to realise
that some people will never change.
They don't know how to.
Not for their own
or someone else's good.
They just cannot.
So stop hurting yourself.
Respect yourself and your peace of
mind enough to take a stand.
Walk away. For your self-worth.

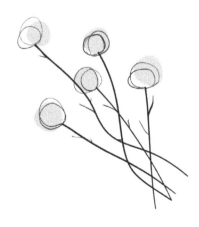

A strong woman battles her way
through the most unjust times.
She strives to keep herself together
in a world that's more often than not
the reason for her pain.
She's tainted, part of her blemished,
her insides even ripped
apart time and time again,
but she never gives up.
But a strong woman is also someone
who allows herself to lay bare and
break. She's also someone who allows
the exertion and ache to surface.
She isn't ashamed.
She is proud of her being.

Breathe.
It's just one of those times again.
It's just making you feel drained.
You are resilient.
You've seen worse.
You can do this.
You can.
Hold yourself together like you
always do.
Just one more time.
Just breathe

That constant turmoil..
Say it, don't say it, say it.. don't
say it
So much to gain and even more to
lose.
The heart aches with the three
words that are almost there.. but
yet far from being spoken ..

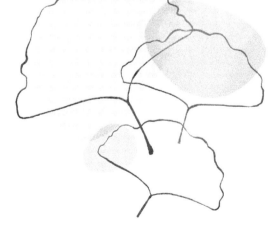

Some cuts run deep...
Some wounds are always fresh..
Some memories are never really
washed away..
These change us.. the person we
were.. to the person we become..
It's seldom out of choice..
Start loving yourself again.. start
today..
Because that's the only way.. that
you'll heal..
But don't ever apologise for
anything that became a part of
your journey..

With every heartbreak, they say a
part of you is taken away..
But you had an identity before all
those pieces fell one by one..
Nobody is worth you letting go of
your true self..
Don't allow yourself to forget that
person.
That's the true you..

Those eyes.. they narrate a tale
that takes a resilient soul to live
through..

Don't ever forget.
We can fake a smile,
But never the look in our eyes.
Those eyes, they spill everything.

Is there any way in which I can walk into my life in a parallel universe where everything is okay and just as it should be? Just the way I imagined it?

If you're hurting - feel it
If you're happy - celebrate it
If you're content - thank your
lucky stars..
Every feeling makes you - you.
Be proud of it.

I know I may not be there yet..
But when I look behind...
I know I've come a long way..
With everything that life showed
me..
I only got wiser.. I only got
stronger..
My will is sturdier than I know..
My pursuit didn't go in vain..
And I know I will get to where I
belong..
I will..

Sometimes, the simplest of words
are misunderstood..

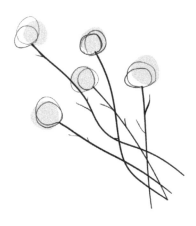

We don't know what we're really
facing, until it's in front of us..
We don't know what we're really
missing, until it's taken away from
us..
We don't know what we're worth,
until we realise our own potential..
Life shows us many shades,
Some dark, others bright..
Let them all sink in, one at a
time..
For every experience makes us
wiser..

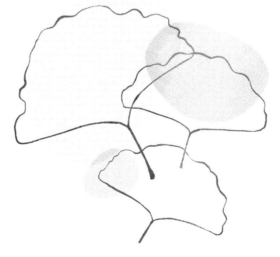

Maybe I've been lying to myself..
Maybe it's actually the reverse..
Maybe the shining sun is actually
the dull gloomy moon..
Maybe sadness is actually
happiness..
Maybe tears are the true sign of
joy..

It's never about how much we have.
It's about how much we felt.

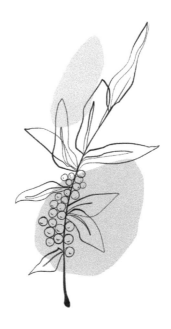

Isn't it ironic that we feel free in love yet caged because sometimes we aren't allowed to express the sheer quantum of it..

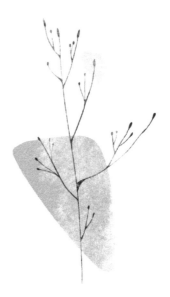

More often than not..
There are two sides of us..
One that's awake and faces the
world..
And the other that lies awake,
pondering and lost in thoughts in
the middle of the night..
Those thoughts are the ones that
make us.. the real version of us..
They are our only truth..

One moment..
It's just that one moment..
It can change everything..
Wars can be won..
People can die..
Peace can be restored..
Love can be lost..
Hearts can be won..
One moment... that's all it takes..

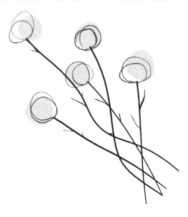

The world around us is changing..
As we speak..
It's not the same..
So be fearless.. carefree.. and
liberated..
Because everything you are.. is
now.. in this moment..

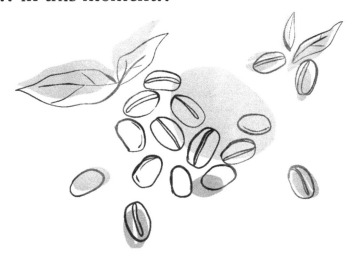

Over the years...she realised that..
Happiness... is a luxury..
It's a myth that exists in her mind,
that's filled with sunlight, green
meadows and nature at it's best..
It's the perfectly painted picture in
her head..
She realised that the secret to her
happiness was a small version of
herself she wrote about..
In a little diary tucked away .. for
her eyes only..
Where she poured her heart out in
everyway..
Those words gave her hope.. that
maybe someday.. the sun would
shine just a little brighter..

The day she realises the force she
has within, the power she exudes,
she will rise..
And when she does, the ocean
won't need the moon to stir
it's tides

Reach into the depths of her soul,
soon you'll find that behind that
mature, wise woman she's just a
little girl, with hopes and dreams
that are waiting to be fulfilled..

The matters of the heart.. they
never make sense..
They're mixed and wired in the
most complex manner imaginable..
But still ..
That doesn't stop us from feeling
that flutter or skipping a
heartbeat..
Knowing full well that the web of
complexity is about to unfold..

You are too precious to give
someone the liberty to change you
the way they wish..
Be in control of your heart and
mind..
That keeps you original..

The heart will beg for more..
It's fuelled by emotions and
feelings..
Nothing will make sense to it..
But there are times when
perhaps, you need to allow your
mind to make the decision..
And more often than not it won't
be the one your heart desires..

No matter how much of an effort
went into taming her, you will
never fully be able to control her
wild spirit and fiery soul..

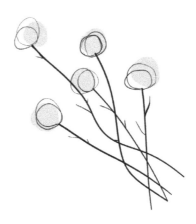

She was made to confront fire and
combat wilder things..

There is a reason why you've seen
what you have..
Been through what you have,
Don't ever stop dreaming and
believing in yourself..

Try me,
Soon enough you'll see I'm
difficult to shatter and impossible
to forget..

Justice.
Important
Extensively delayed
Often misused and sometimes
non-existent

We toil..
We strive..
Sometimes even bleed..
Just be sure it is all worth
something..
Else you've just lost a lifetime of
moments that are never coming
back..

With some people,
Something just clicks..
Don't box the feeling by
definition..
Good samaritans are hard to find..
So just go with it..

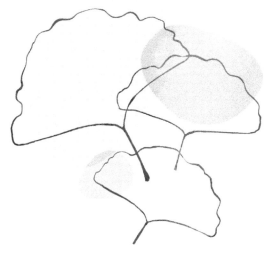

More often than not,
A familiar shadow looks at me..
Gazing from a distance..sometimes
it mocks me..
I finally took the courage to walk
upto it and confront my fear..
What I was looking at, was me..
Just in the form of who I wanted
to be..
Staring back into the eyes of who
I'd become..

You know who you are..
You know what you are..
Never settle..

When it stops making a
difference..
There may be a reason to worry..

Ego is always self-destructing..
Nothing good ever comes out of
it..
Treat it like the side of you..
You yourself would never want to
know..

Don't differentiate..
The problem arises when we look
down on professions we don't
aspire to..
Remember, no job is too small.

Live the kind of life,
That lives on..
In numerous hearts,
Even after you depart..

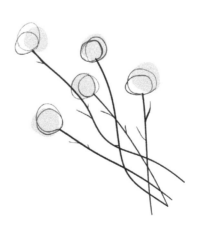

You are most alive in your sleep..
That's the only time your
subconscious self is awake..

Sometimes, it's okay to be quiet
and not have the last say,
They may feel you were weak,
What they'll realise much later is
that you were wise..

Being strong is exhausting,
But when you climb that
mountain..
The breathtaking view on the
other side..
Makes it all worth it..

We succumb to our weaknesses
more than rising to our strengths,
Imagine what it would be like if
the equation was reversed..

Nothing annoys the evil ones more than the reaction of a calm and composed mind..

Only when you dare to question
the 'Why'..
And are ready to accept the
answer..whatever the answer
maybe..
Are you likely to reach a place
called 'Closure'..

I don't think we will ever learn
where to draw the line for the ones
we love..
Because no matter what, giving is
all we know..

It's your life..
Your blank canvas..
Choose your colours and strokes wisely

Verses n Sonnets

ABOUT THE AUTHOR

Nupur Gadkari, graduated from Warwick Business School, UK, in the year of the Global Financial Crisis and has since made 'Challenge Accepted' her motto in life. Despite taking on the responsibility of looking after her much younger siblings at the age of 14, she's never let anything hold her back. She's built an impressive career in Marketing over the past 15 years with global brands such as, IMG Worldwide, Castrol-BP, Mattel and Walt Disney.

A proud Mumbai-city girl, she was always a non-conformist. She never saw herself 'settling down' to a life of domesticity and was always seen as a dreamer who never stopped believing. This is probably why she's been able to make such an impact wherever she's been.

It's against this backdrop that this book came to life. Through the years of turmoil, relationship ups and downs as well as challenges at home and at work, she turned to writing poetry as way of healing. To her surprise, her thoughts seemed to resonate with so many and this rapidly helped her grow a large and loyal social media following.

Nupur has broken the stereotypes and made a success of everything she's set her heart and mind to. As well as a stellar corporate career, she is also an artist, chef and emotive author. Someone who is able to express in words, what we all feel; love, life, joy, sadness; the whole spectrum.

It is her hope that this book, becomes a 'friend' for readers to 'lean on' through the roller coaster of life.

Follow us:
@versesnsonnets

Lightning Source UK Ltd.
Milton Keynes UK
UKHW011829200821
389211UK00001B/164

9 781637 920961